FIRST AID FOR SORROW

Marian McDonald

Dedicated to: John, husband of 70
years

Inspired by: Tom, friend of 5 years

Arranged by: Margaret McDonald
Lemrise, daughter

CONTENTS

INTRODUCTION

I believe all of us have a drawer, box or closet corner where we collect mementos. Cards and letters from loved ones or maybe a diary of many years. We go through the pile from time to time and are left with a smile and renewed warmth for the senders.

Mom had such a box that I retrieved from her bedside table after her death. Five inches deep and loaded with handwritten notes; greeting cards; letters; poems; newspaper clippings; diary entries. Some dated back eighty-seven years and some as recent as last year.

Well, I began sifting through the old crumbling papers, post-it notes, college ruled paper and fine stationery. I read each page and assumed I was experiencing the feelings Mom felt. Through my encounter of the saved keepsakes, I felt near to Mom.

Repeatedly, the words important to her and dear to her heart fed my need to have her close once more.

I want to share with you, the reader, what has become a healing process for me. Don't know what to do with the pile of papers that once belonged to your loved one? Read them. Read them again. Understand why these papers needed to be kept in a special place. It can be therapy for a grieving spirit.

Margaret McDonald Lemrise

FIRST AID FOR SORROW

BY

MARIAN MCDONALD

CHAPTER ONE

RELATIONSHIPS REMEMBERED

MOM

Is it wrong to pray for darkness to come?

And steal from her eyes the morning sun?

Is it wrong to ask that Death stealthily creep?

And unburden her soul while she's asleep?

What her eyes behold now are sights unreal-

The terror and loneliness only old people feel.

Her mind rarely grasps the present time-

It lingers always in years behind.

Her face once shining from beauty within

Is scarred by lonely years without him.

We hope for life in the sick who are young,

But hope is gone when life's day is done.

Is it wrong to pray for Death to come?

That old, dimmed eyes see a new day's sun?

She, herself, prays she'll soon be free

From the horror her life has grown to be.

So is it wrong for me, her daughter, to pray
That the Lord of Light lift her soul away
And leave that body old and worn
To the keeper of Graves and the few who will mourn?

THE FISHES BANQUET

(Written to DAD in 1930)

When pa goes fishin', he just sits

And burns up in the sun;

He wipes his brow as sweat rolls down;

The fish have all the fun.

They swim about him gracefully

Nibbling his clams and flies;

Getting nice and fat and juicy

For the next who comes and tries.

By an act of fate, to catch one once

Somehow pa did contrive,

But an innocent fish three inches long

Is a measly meal for five.

A POEM FOR MY SISTER

God has filled my life with beautiful
things

That will live in my heart evermore.

Often when I'm weary and need some
smiles,

I turn the clock back to days of yore.

And there we are - two young girls
again

In pretty dresses that our dear Mom
made, Walking to Pope Park with our
brown-bag lunch -

Tuna fish sandwiches and pink
lemonade.

Sunday, after church, was a day of rest.

We couldn't play with friends, but still had fun.

We cut out paper dolls from, Montgomery Ward,

Or played "Church" - you were the priest, I was a nun.

You made sweet music with your piano -

Opera, classical, hymns, any song.

I sang along in a world all our own.

Golden hours together. Days never seemed long.

No TV. No car, but we weren't bored

With activities in church, school work, friends,

A library to hike to; books to read; our youth was "special", but everything ends.

Time passed. You brought me to meet King's Daughters.

They give help to the needs "In Jesus' name".

They'll always be our friends and part of our lives,

Wish you were here. Nothing seems quite the same.

Though we're old, in our 80's, we still had fun -

Food shopping - the pleasure couldn't be beat!

With our purchases safely stacked in the car,

We did what we do best - found a place to eat.

Now in Georgia, in Cappy's watchful care,

You will get your eye drops and pills on time.

No more snow-drifts or treacherous, slippery ice.

I'd better close. I'm running out of rhyme.

I know someday we'll met again.

I wonder when. There is only "One" can tell.

But whatever God has in store for us,

One thing is sure, "He doeth all thigs well".

CHAPTER TWO
DIARIES HEAL

MAY 8, 2011

A day that will live in my memory forevermore. My dear husband, John, my companion, friend, confident died; left me to travel life's highway alone. I spent that entire night, and many thereafter in the darkness asking questions that crowded in without answers. How could I go on living without him? Why him? Why didn't God take me? John was the better person.

All the memories too kept me awake. John and I were married 70 years, but were friends when we were kids-met in Sunday school 83 years ago; he was 11 ½ , I was

10. We were good friends from day one so the memories go back to the carefree days of childhood. So many things passed in review and so many tears fell. They blurred these beautiful older, golden days of yesteryears.

I saw the things the two of us loved so well- the Sunday school class where we met, the park path where we strolled and kissed while the silvery moon smiled down, meadows, hills, school friends, our wonderful parents.

Where will this road end that I travel each day?

I've searched the scriptures to see what will be.

There's a dark, unknown valley I must transverse

Before heaven opens its portals to me.

The psalmist had no fear of the valley,

Because the Lord was always by his side.

He knew that if he followed the Lord

In His house forever he would abide.

Like the psalmist, the Lord is my Shepard, too.

When from green pastures and still waters I roam

Always the Lord finds me and brings me back

To the path that leads me to my heavenly home.

DEAR DIARY

Yes, Irene, sometimes we feel helpless in the face of sorrow and say, "There is nothing I can do or say to ease the pain of someone coping with the death of her life-long mate." Then we stop to think - we can always pray. We know from experience that prayer is a source of power that gives strength, comfort and peace. We want you to know our prayers are with you.

You and Ray had a special love that has stood the test of time. Now that all-enfolding love will bridge the distance between heaven and earth. All the great times you enjoyed together will become precious memories to give your dreams a cheery glow when nights are dark and dreary. You will keep a candle lit in your heart forever for Ray while you are apart.

We are thrilled to see how springtime creeps silently into the country side again. The once apparently dead branches are alive with greenery. All around are symbols of Easter as life begins anew. Somewhere from deep inside come the words, "I am the resurrection and the life".

We will never forget Ray or his dear lovely wife.

PARTY TIME

My 81st birthday was glorious. Daughters came for breakfast and began installing the decorations, balloons, flowers and favors. The décor was intended to set the theme of the party which was "Youth". I don't know how many visited during the day - some for cake and ice cream only - others for games and social fun, etc.

Margaret made a beautifully decorated cake with about two candles. I was told to make a wish and everyone sang "Happy Birthday" and then the children were instructed to help Grammie blow out the candles. In a flash the table was surrounded by yelling, enthusiastic youngsters and a mini hurricane followed with pleas to light the candles again and then another hurricane ensued.

When we finally got to cutting the cake, I removed the frosting, stating for caloric reasons, but it was really sanitation problems that worried me.

WHY SO LONG?

Often wonder why God has let me live so long. Have decided it is because I still have lots to learn about pain, patience, kindness and love. There is also a lot of good hard work left in me and I have to be here to help John. He has had two mini strokes and a five way heart by-pass, but right now he is doing well.

I'll keep my eyes steadfastly on 100. I'm tough enough!

STAR SPANGLED BANNER

July 4th

Of course we had quite a few guests today. Johnnie grilled some hot dogs and when I saw them I said, "I can't possibly eat one of those - they are at least a foot long!" He told me to do the best I could and do you know what? I managed to squeeze it in somewhere, plus a sampling of nearly everything else. Esther was featuring a new mac and cheese dish that was excellent. I never met any food that I do not like!

John ate two of those gigantic hot dogs. He didn't meet any food that he didn't like. I think he should enter a hot dog eating contest. I'm sure (in his age bracket) he would come home with a shining trophy and, probably, some kind of painful intestinal distress. Right now he is supplementing his bedtime snack with "Tums". I guess if we can sit up and take nourishment at our ages, there is hope for some kind of a future.

Think I'll stock up on those hot dogs and a goodly supply of "Tums".

EYE SURGERY

Life has been great! No matter which way the eye operation turns out, memory has painted some treasured scenes on the walls of my mind. Their colors never fade and they are mine forever.

NOVEMBER 2005

The weather is beautiful - cool, clear, invigorating. Makes me feel like doing house cleaning, or sitting and soaking up the sunshine. I decided on the latter, so here I am, sitting on the back porch enjoying the fresh, nippy November air and the end of summer beauty. It is really autumn, but everything is late. John and Micki are raking leaves and so are lots of neighbors. Lots of them have fallen (leaves, of course, not the rakers). Usually by this time in the year the trees are bare, but they are still colorful.

All the glee down in the yard lured me over to join the workers. Many nice memories there with kids jumping in the piles of leaves. Wish I could do that with them, but feel blessed just to be around and remember.

DECEMBER 2005

At the end of our property is a row of 30' pine trees. These are my out-door Christmas trees during December. They are very special because God himself will decorate them with that fluffy white stuff that gleans in the sunshine and sparkles in the moonlight - snow - and not one branch will be forgotten. Sometimes He sends an ice storm and the trees turn to glass. They snap, crackle and pop when the sun gets a bit warm and ice falls to the ground. Some things are so beautiful you don't just see them with your eyes, you feel a thrill and tingle deep in your

soul and know that God is the reason
for such beauty.

ANNIVERSARY GIFT

Micki's family has a swimming pool,
trampoline, and lots of stuff to charm a
swarm of kids. We had a gorgeous
cake and opened presents.

The kids gave us a trip to "Rydin' Hi" -
a dude ranch in upper New York State.
We didn't ride the horses, but went on
hay rides, boat trips around the lake,
enjoyed the sauna and heated pool,
went fishing, attended a steak

barbeque; 10:00 PM hot dog party, a pizza party, movies, bingo, hikes, etc.

My heart was enchanted by the beauty everywhere. The hills and fields were fairy lands, sweet and still green. The azure skies had lots of fluffy clouds; and leaves, just turning colors, were bright and gay. All these are gifts I fondly treasure in my memory tonight.

CANE

I love my cane. It's like a magic wand - people are always offering me help. For instance: We voted at the school and it was so crowded the line went almost around the gymnasium. I was ready to go home, but some lady came to me and said, "I'm near the front with my husband, why don't you get in front of us?" I said, "That would be nice, but this is my husband, John. He is older than I am and we are inseparable."

She laughed and invited us both. We were out of there in minutes. The thought does occur to me that the cane isn't magic, but that I look pitifully decrepit.

THANKSGIVING

Thanksgiving turkey has lost some of its special awe that it had when I was a child. Modern stores sell them every day, frozen, fresh, legs, breasts - any parts, and there is no such thing as seasonal veggies. The awesome part is that every heart seems to turn homeward for the holidays and the feeling of love and friendship has no words that describe the wonder of it all.

The meal was great. Next day I had a hangover - not from alcohol, but the kind from too much food that appears above the belt.

FRIENDSHIP

Micki stopped in the room to say, "Hi". She is going to stay overnight and plans to bake some Christmas cookies. I told her I was thinking to write my "good friend, Howard a greeting". She went upstairs with a question, "How can anyone carry on a friendship when they see each other only once in twenty years and live so far away?"

I say that some folk move away and then they are gone. When they are gone, they are gone. But true friends can leave and still remain. No erasing, blurring, or forsaking.

Distance isn't really a barrier to friendship, it adds a new dimension to it. Friends help to shape me by their influence, example and encouragement. I don't know if my life has much influence on my friends, but I do know Howard's wit, wisdom and patience made a profound difference in mine. Our mutual experience at Veeder- Root still binds us. Christmas is a good time to thank him for walking friendship's path with me.

TRABECULECTOMY

Because of glaucoma, the pressure in my eyes was building up - especially serious in the left eye. The surgeon inserted a flap to drain fluid so the pressure could drop. It was not a success. As the pressure climbs, my eyesight will get dimmer.

I am enjoying the sight I now have. Baking, writing, puzzles. For now it is "Funsville".

NOT FEELING WELL

The summer of 2006 was a rugged, up-hill climb. In June my tongue hurt and became very swollen. Within two days, my whole mouth had some kind of canker sores. I looked like a witch, could eat only a liquid diet, couldn't wear my false teeth and worse of all, I could hardly talk - a great catastrophe for any female.

My doc tried "cures", none of which worked. He then sent me to a dentist who sent me to another dentist, who sent me to an oral surgeon. I had swab tests, blood tests, x-rays, teeth relined, pills, wafers to chew every four hours. Even set the alarm at night to chew more wafers. After 2 ½ months I was finally stamped "cured" of some kind of fungus that nobody can

imagine where it came from. I felt
dangerously ill - couldn't stop losing weight.
However; now I feel dangerously well!!!

BYE BYE BOOK

When I was sick, I had plenty of time to
read over the book that I have spent years
and years, off and on, writing. I finally
made a decision:

One morning I stood looking out our front
room window as the Windsor sanitation
truck turned our ashcan upside down and
dumped the contents into the rubbish bin.
Then I watched the truck disappear around
the corner with my shredded manuscript and
the rest of the garbage.

I can't get that day out of my mind. It was raining hard. Just the fitting weather for such a bitter parting with all my created characters that seemed like family.

Why did I do away with my book if I felt so bad about destroying it? Because I don't want anyone to think that possibly the heroine was I - that I was writing about myself. Some of Maggie's adventures were mine, but mostly the book was a product of a very over-active imagination. I don't want people to think I even thought of such stuff. Maggie did have some encounters that turned her life around and she reformed. With morals of the world being what they are today, I think the book was destined to be a best seller. The book is where it belongs-with the garbage.

SNOW

One morning a couple of weeks ago I got up and looked out the window to check the weather. My heart beat fast at the beautiful scene before me. During the night snow fell and made my world a sparkling, winter wonderland. Snowflakes, great big ones, whirled and danced in the wind on their downward flight. The dull landscape was sparkling; bare trees were laden with that glistening, white stuff. Not a branch or twig was forgotten.

Snowstorms open the gates of memory. I sat in front of the picture window and dreamed of long ago storms when I was a little girl and made a snowman with my sister and brother. It was nice thinking about them, seeing them again, and doing the things we used to do.

As a teenager I went skating with John. Snowflakes made the day more beautiful. Skating was never one of my talents and sometimes I fell or got pretty shaky, but there was John, ready to pick me up, provide a steady arm, and point me in the right direction - just as he has for 66 years whenever life has thrown me some unsteadying punches.

SLEEPOVER

Two little great grandchildren are sleeping over tonight. They are supposed to be sleeping, but sounds like they are fighting instead. I dash to separate them.

Why is it that it always seems to be the boys that have to punch and kick? These two are always fighting, but always want to be together. It never seems to affect their love for each other. It only affects my patience.

ACHES AND PAINS

When I was young, I wished old folks wouldn't talk so much about their aches and pains and wondered if they realized how boring it was. Now that I am "old folk" I realize that aches and pains are a very large part of our lives, and people like to talk about a subject they know lots about.

I have a couple of aches and pains, but I believe that if you talk about your troubles and tell them o'er and o'er, the Lord will think you like them and proceed to send you more.

SO AGILE

Jeannette and Bradd returned recently from a trip to Florida. They stopped in earlier today for lunch with us.

She was telling how Bradd's aunt came bouncing out of the house to greet them.

The aunt rides a horse everyday. "Ma, you would be amazed at how she bounces around and she is 81 years old."

I sensed a comparison and felt a need to defend my inability to perform those activities. No, I don't bounce around or out of houses, except, maybe on icy days. Horseback riding is definitely an "I can't", but then, I am only 77 and who knows what I will be doing in four years from now. I may be very athletic and wiry.

Jeannette must have sensed the jealousy. I try to admire great physical feats in 81 year olds, but it really is jealousy. My daughter planted a kiss on my nose. She always says the right thing, "You're more fun, Mom".

JOYOUS ADDITIONS

I wonder what fears and memories are tucked way back in the little girls' young brains, and what the kiddies have seen and experienced. Johnnie and Wendy and the girls trimmed their tree last night. It was the first tree the children had ever had and they were ecstatic.

They already call Johnnie and Wendy, "Daddy" and "Mommy" and they call John and me, "Gramps and Grammie". No one ever told them to. We are hoping our family will be increased by two grandchildren all at one time.

Every day that dawns anew brings blessings heaped on blessings. Everywhere we look,

God's blessings are there and my heart overflows.

CHAPTER 3

BIRTHDAYS COUNT; ANNIVERSARYS BUILD

BIRTHDAY

30

I hate to think about old age

When my step is feeble and slow;

My teeth extracted or decayed -

My hair a bank of snow.

I hate to think about wrinkles

And looking like a prune,

But the way time speeds by I guess

Old age will get me soon.

I like me as I am right now.

I wish the hands of time would stay.

With aching joints and eyesight dim -

I'm not going to like me that way.

Right now the blazing flame of youth

Within my heart burns bright.

Old age hasn't got me yet

Though I'm thirty years old tonight.

BIRTHDAY

<u>70</u>

I've nearly reached my allotted

Three score years and ten.

Often I'm asked the question,

"Don't you wish you were young
again?"

Sometimes I hear youth's laughter;

See their faces all aglow,

And suddenly I'm a girl again

In the world I used to know.

I see my friends, the church, and the
school.

I can smell Mom's apple pies.

My folks were poor, but I felt rich;

I owned all the sun in the skies.

I can't forget the boy next door,

Or the picnics we shared in the park,

And warmth of stolen kisses

On the back porch stairs after dark.

I love my trips down memory lane

Back to haunts long ago,

But trade my todays for yester years?

The answer is a definite, "NO!"

Youth can't match all the treasures

That are part of my life today -

Grown-up children and grandchildren;

Dearer than life are they.

I find God's love is everywhere,

With steadfast faith I am blest.

Youth must plant the proper seed

Or age won't enjoy the harvest.

I have a word for young folks
Concerning the seeds that you sow.
"The more of love you give away,
The more it will bloom and grow.

BIRTHDAY

73

Someone said, "Old folk are beautiful!"

I was young then and didn't agree.

I looked at changes the years can make

And dreaded what time would do to
me.

I said, "Beauty describes only young
folk;

Like a bonnie lass with unlined face,

A smile that reflects carefree
happiness;

Her slim form, a silhouette of grace."

Now, looking through older, wiser eyes

I find old faces hold beauty, indeed,

Most glow with love grown strong
through years

And great faith, once small as a
mustard seed.

I think each of us is responsible

For our looks as older we grow.

Has our faith and kindness grown also?

Does the love in our hearts overflow?

If we hate, criticize, and complain a lot,

If we let life's problems get us down,

Then old age wrinkles won't be
character lines.

Instead we'll turn into a big, ugly
frown.

Cosmetics and face lifts won't do the trick.

Beauty is soul stuff. It's something divine.

While you are still young -

Love, beautiful friend of mine.

BIRTHDAY

<u>82</u>

I like to sit and talk – remembering.

Memory keeps folks near when they're far apart.

It spans the deep abyss of life and death,

Its magic brings cheer to a saddened heart.

Five children left footprints on memory's lane

They have brought us joy all life through,

And take good care of the old folk.

Scenes of their childhood oft pass in review.

Father Time scribbled deep lines on my
face,

Took the pep from my step, turned my
hair gray.

For 82 years I've roamed life's
highroads,

I'm a bit weary, I've come a long way.

BIRTHDAY

<u>85</u>

A sunbeam, touching my cheek, said to
me,

"Wake up. It's morning. Get up. Look
alive!

The sun shines; birds sing; outdoors
calls; it's spring!

Celebrate, Birthday Girl! You're
eighty-five."

We partied outdoors that beautiful day

Among the guests, great grandkids -
quite a few.

One picked a dandelion-grass bouquet,

Hugged me and whispered, "Great
Gram, I love you."

A wee laddie called, "Gram, can you do this?"

Then stood on his head, feet straight in the air.

I replied, "No, haven't tried it of late,

Guess I'll just rock in my old rocking chair."

Youngsters and oldsters sang "Happy Birthday"

Very loud, with small tots very off key.

A solemn thought crossed my mind while they sang,

"How many birthdays will there be?"

Sober thoughts don't stay long with children near.

We sang, played games, they drew pictures of me.

Time spent with loved ones is never enough.

How precious are photos and memory?

Too soon 'twas over - we said our "goodbyes"

And a golden sun set on my perfect day.

But in the shadows, more solemn thoughts lurked

With no children left to chase them away.

Eighty-five! I'm old. Where'd all the time go?

I'm nearer heaven than I've been before.

Closer to that place prepared just for
me

Where dear ones, long gone, again I
will see.

Tonight I long for Mom's gentle touch,

The love in her eyes; the smile on her
face.

Thank you, God, for the loved ones
here on earth,

Who make this old world a beautiful
place?

I wish John and I could leave together,

Hand in hand when it's our time to go,

But first I hope God sends me more
birthdays,

Not a whole lot - maybe fifteen or so.

I'll be ready, in my one hundredth year

To explore the "larger life" beyond
here!

BIRTHDAY

<u>86</u>

Thank you God for another nice
birthday.

You've given me lots of them-now
eighty-six.

Good health, too, I've got some pains
here and there,

But nothing a handful of pills won't fix.

Birthdays make some old folks sand
and depressed,

To me they are fun days. I enjoy all of
mine.

There is always a party and if it rains,

My guests know how to make their
own sunshine.

BIRTHDAY

<u>87</u>

I've come a long way on this highway
of life,

Been traveling many long years,
eighty-seven.

I love where I've been and will love
what's ahead,

This road leads to the golden gates of
heaven.

I love where I'm at on this highway
today.

John is here, friends and family are
near.

In our comfy house nestled mid trees
and flowers,

Filled with love and some "stuff" that I
hold dear.

We have been blessed with five kind,
loving children.

They've brought lots of joy to our
humble abode.

The blessings are mine hear and now.

The best is yet to come - at the end of
the road.

BIRTHDAY

<u>89</u>

I've journeyed far on life's highway,
with its many back roads to roam.

Been traveling now for eighty nine
years, destination, my heavenly home.

I have reached a place called Old Age,
well known for its sorrow and pain;

Steps are feeble and slow, eyesight
dim. There's lots of wheelchairs, many
a cane.

Folks say there's no gold in the Golden
Years, some say there is no reason to
smile.

I say it's time to count our blessings! I
like it here; hope to stay a while.

Old Age is filled with lovely
things...Friends and family aren't far
away;

John is here in our cozy nest. God sends showers of blessings each day.

Our back yard is full of miracles, each season brings new beauty and glow;

A robin's nest, a summer breeze, red leaves, I am a kid again in wind-blown snow.

Oldsters are entertained anytime, with our cell phones, computers, TVs.

I love to read, write, sew, do household chores and try out on John new recipes.

Because our children are kind and caring, we walk with a much lighter load.

They bring us sunshine and happiness, and brighten life's long, winding road.

Sometimes I wander down memory lane, back to the good old days of yore.

Back to the house where I grew up and John was the boy I loved next door.

Feels good to be young, if only in dreams, close to those I once loved tenderly.

Most have died, but still live in my heart. It's God's comforting sweet mystery.

Doomed to a cold and silent tomb...Some think that's what our future will be.

The Bible says not so and that's good news, for a little old lady like me.

There's a larger life out there somewhere, faith says death is not the end.

I'll go to a greater adventure and not alone, I'll go with a friend.

Jesus is with me, has been since the start. When we move on remember, no tears.

I'm glad I reached Old Age, it's amazing, there's gold everywhere in our Golden years.

BIRTHDAY

<u>90</u>

With prayer and praise and joy I
watched

As the Eastern sky showed a streak of
gray;

And I felt a thrill, as I said out loud,

"Birthday girl, you're ninety years old
today."

I gave thanks to God for letting me live

In His beautiful world for so long.

Thus my day began - a smile on my
face -

In my heart a happy song.

Memory tip-toed in on a fragrant
breeze

And carried me back to the long ago;

To the music and laughter of my youth
-

Back to places and faces I used to
know.

I visited in dreams where I grew up -

The school, church, the old home so
sweet and fair.

Dear parents and siblings are long
gone,

But I feel their presence everywhere.

The freckled-face boy who lived next
door;

Grew up to be the love of my life.

I never thought any day could be
happier,

Than the day I became his loving wife.

The days did get happier as the years slipped by

With four sweet baby girls - one rough, tough boy.

Somehow these tiny babes smuggled in

A life-time supply of love and joy.

Today my children gave me a party.

With their expertise, it was a huge success.

They promised a "special surprise event",

It would be so unique, no one could guess.

The party began with talk and hors d'oeuvres,

"We've got to go", someone said suddenly.

My daughter walked me to the street.

"The surprise has arrived", she
explained to me.

Up the street came a van, very slowly,

From a boom-box marching music
played.

This was the start of an epic production
-

A heart-warming; spine-tingling,
parade.

Two sturdy great grandsons held a huge
sign;

"Happy Birthday" it read, "90 years -
WOW!

Then came grandchildren, more great
grands too!

They all kept in step, I don't know how.

Next, more relatives - husbands and wives -

Even dear neighbors and many a friend!

They waved, shouted, tooted horns, laughed and cheered.

Next came the sad part; it all had to end!!!

The party is over; I should feel "Done In".

I feel GREAT. No aches, pains or other ills.

I'm feeling young and, oh, so happy,

If old folk had more parties - we'd need fewer pills.

Now I near the end of my lovely day,

When the world grows hushed and serene.

I love sunset time with my Prince Charming.

Though the years have been many, I'm still his Queen.

BIRTHDAY

<u>96</u>

I well remember that day in May. A
day to rejoice,

It was my birthday.

Oh, what a party we had, a feast was
prepared.

Tables groaned beneath the weight,

Two candles revealed my age, an
awesome ninety eight.

Forty three family and friends came to
celebrate,

They sure knew how to make my party
great.

They filled the house with laughter and
glee,

Everyone enjoyed the heartwarming
comradery.

The scintillating conversation made the time pass fast and pleasantly.

Two great, granddaughters brought much beauty to this event,

With guitars and sweet voices, they provided entertainment.

They took a bit of poetry written by me,

And set it to music, composing a lovely melody.

Their music mesmerizes me,

It is always beautiful, and so are they.

I said at the start of my party that by the end of the day,

I would be worn out and done-in; not so.

At 11:00 pm I was eating another piece of birthday cake, Basking in the party's afterglow.

I found out at that time I had forgotten
my daily pills.

Hadn't taken even one. Guess I was
having too much fun.

Guess there is one thing I could say---

If I had more parties, I could throw the
pills away.

BIRTHDAY

<u>97</u>

"What do you want for your birthday?"
I am asked,

And I really do not know.

I have everything; and there is no place
I want to go.

But to my children I have a few words
to say,

I am writing this poem in your honor
today.

Today is my birthday. I am ninety-
seven.

That is old, very old. I belong in
Heaven.

But not so, here I am with appetite
hearty,

Dressed in my best and ready to party.

I took care of five babies long, long
ago;

Today they take care of me, my step
feeble and slow.

All my children are senior citizens
now.

Keeping me happy and healthy, they
have the know-how.

They fill my world with music and
laughter,

Enough happiness and love to last
forever after.

A cord of love that naught can sever

Binds us together, forever and ever.

I can't escape one solemn thought

That sometimes comes over me.

I wonder how many more birthdays
there will be.

It is in God's hands. He does what is best.

I do not need to know.

With a thankful heart for all of my days.

Back to life's journey I go

I am heading for Heaven beyond this sunset somewhere.

My Darling Five with their loving care

Make me feel like I am already there.

BIRTHDAY

<u>98</u>

This morning I was awakened by a
sweet melody,

The song of a wee bird in the nearby
maple tree.

I rushed to the opened window to get as
near as I could be,

To the little songster that sang so
prettily.

The sun greeted me there with a warm
hug and kiss,

"Howdy", said he, "Hope your day is
filled with happiness."

When I was young, I thought old age
was something to fear and dread,

Now I know each season has its beauty;
greater adventure lies just ahead.

High up in the trees a frisky, May breeze was playing tag and dancing with the leaves.

Then down to my window to rumple up my hair, while perfume from roses and lilies permeated the air.

In the beauty of the morning, God seemed very near,

His thoughts, like the wind, blew across my mind and these words fell upon my ear:

"I love you my child, and want you to know, I am with you always, wherever you go.

It is your happy birthday, an awesome ninety eight! You have a long day ahead, lots to celebrate."

I could smell coffee and bacon sizzling in the pan.

I ate, listened to music, typed; then it was time to start my children's exercise plan.

They say if I just eat, sleep and sit I will soon grow old and pitifully decrepit.

So they planned for me some exercise designed to keep me fit.

I take my companions' arm and down the driveway we stroll.

When I reach the third house, I'm halfway to my goal.

Back at the driveway my children have put a "comfy" chair at the top,

They know my body will be racked with pain and I'll be ready to drop.

Folks say our driveway is a very slight incline. I disagree; their point of view does not correspond with mine.

The driveway is steep; a real muscle test. I know how Edmond Hillary felt, the day he conquered Mt. Everest.

The kids made a feast, guests brought food too; tables groaned 'neath the weight.

Forty three people came to my noon time lunch; they just ate, ate and ate.

More about my birthday party, I'll write at Christmas time,

My fingers are weary, I need a nap and I've also run out of rhyme.

****

Tonight I sit alone in my room, deep in thought.

Thanking God for the joy and love

My ninety-eight years of life have brought.

I rejoice and I am exceedingly glad,

My five children are the greatest
Any mom anywhere ever had.
If I didn't have them where would I be?
What would I do, Where would I go?
Hope I never have to know!

50th WEDDING ANNIVERSAY

Hartford Courant

August 1990

Marian and John McDonald

Marian and John McDonald of Windsor
celebrated their 50th wedding anniversary
August 25th with family and friends.
Members of the original wedding party who
attended included Clarence and Marjorie
Taylor of East Hartford, John Williams of
East Hartford, and Michael and Agnes

Majer of California. The McDonalds plan a
motor tour of Maine and Nova Scotia in
honor of the event.

65th WEDDING ANNIVERSAY

Hartford Courant

August 2005

On Sunday, August 28th Marian and John McDonald celebrated 65 years of marriage at their home in Windsor. The 45 guests attending their Anniversary Open House, arranged by their 5 children, were grand and great-grandchildren, as well as brother, sister, cousin and friends of the couple.

Now retired Reverend Mason Ellison, cousin of the bride, offered grace prior to lunch and after the cake was cut. Mrs. McDonald read a poem she composed for the occasion. Marriage, love, family home and growing old together were the theme of her script.

Marian and John were married in Hartford on August 31, 1940 and have lived in Windsor since 1950. John is retired from the Underwood and USPs and Marian's professional life was at the Veeder-Root in Hartford.

John and I celebrated our 65th wedding anniversary the end of August. Above is a copy of a write-up Margaret sent to the Courant. Among the guests was our new great-grandson, Raymond Andrew Lemrise, only a couple of weeks old.

If I hadn't lived to be so old, I would have missed a couple of awesome times in life - my 65th anniversary party and greeting so many great-grandchildren as they arrive into this wonderful life.

70th WEDDING ANNIVERSAY

Hartford Courant

August 2010

August 2010

Not much money, but we have great wealth!
Our marriage brought riches more precious
than gold.
A house full of children – their love and
laughter,
Sweet mem'ries forever to have and to
hold."

Marian

On August 29, 2010 John and Marian

Sargent McDonald will celebrate their 70th

Wedding Anniversary at a family picnic at their home in Windsor. The couple has five children. Three daughters: Jeannette (married to Bradd Tompkins), Margaret Lemrise, Esther Cabral and Micki McDonald. They have one son, John (married to Wendy McNeill). The couple has 12 grandchildren and 21 great grandchildren.

John and Marian met 82 years ago in Sunday school. Marian worked for 27 years at Veeder-Root. John worked at the Underwood Typewriter Co. and then as a letter carrier at the U.S. Post Office.

The couple comment on their favorite things as follows:

We like hanging out in our favorite place--home--where friends and family stop in almost every day; every Saturday is Pinochle Party time, and John tends his tomato patch (which has produced tomatoes of remarkable size and quantity).

We enjoy our tapes of the sweet, old-time, romantic songs and the old familiar hymns. We like TV sports and political programs; TV games, reading and refreshing naps outdoors in the gazebo.

All of our children, including our son, are excellent cooks, and though we enjoy restaurants, better still are the homemade meals the children deliver 3 or 4 times a week, sometimes with the announcement, "We have come to work." The housework gets done, the lawn mowed, and broken things get mended, etc…. Life is sweet.

Our marriage has been showered with

blessings!

CHAPTER FOUR
FAITH IS THE KEY

FAITH

At first faith is a fragile thing.

You must nurture it with care.

Read the Bible - go to church,

And spend lots of time in prayer.

Sometimes in storms faith falters,

But stop praying? - no never!

When the sun comes out as it always does,

You'll find you are stronger than ever.

Sometimes the road has been rocky,

But my life has been truly grand.

I married my childhood sweetheart.

We've traveled far hand in hand.

Together we have climbed our mountain;

Looked back on a lovely view;

Gone down the backside - still hand in hand,

And found the valley beautiful too.

Sometimes I like to sit and think

Of how it's going to be

When I hear that "special" knock on the
door

That no one can hear, but me.

Jesus Himself will lead me forth!

I'll hardly believe my eyes

Cause I won't step out onto Timber Lane;

I'll walk straight into Paradise.

I'll kneel before my Savior,

Look up into his wonderful face,

Then I'll fully understand His words -

"I'll go to prepare you a place."

There'll be a glorious reunion

With loved ones who've gone before.

Greater adventure awaits me

When Jesus flings wide the door!

When death comes and leaves empty paces

And night is full of despair and gloom,

Faith whispers of "joy in the morning"

And points to our Lord's empty tomb.

'Twas at that tomb Christ spoke to Mary

We too can hear the Master's voice -

"Why weepest, thou?" Because He lives.

Our friends' live also; sad hearts rejoice!!

In pain; in grief - doubt not God's love.

Someday all things we'll understand.

Until that time, like little children

We must hold tightly to Our Father's hand.

It was dawn, the sky all pink and gold.

In a cold damp tomb, silent and dark as the
night,

A dead figure stirred ~ a great stone rolled
away.

And our crucified lord walked out into the light.

When I think how he took my place on the cross

And died for me, I feel a tear drop start.

These are precious moments spent with you Dear Lord.

I'll keep them with other treasures. Safe in my heart.

OUR PRAYER

Dear Heavenly Father, You pour your beauty and love into every

season of life. Spring is beautiful and so is old age. John and I thank you for the privilege of living to see our children grown and with children of their own…awesome grandchildren!!

We ask thy blessing, not only on this food, but upon all the happy folks gathered here for this 80th birthday celebration. No matter how young or old, we need your love and guidance.

In Jesus name we ask for both.

Amen

I BELIEVE IN MIRACLES

Although wintry flakes fell on the world last night,

Miracles of spring warm the hearts of everyone.

The spirit of God moves in the cold, dark ground,

And green blades push their way out-back in the sun.¬¬

There is no death` after winter there is spring,

A sleeping earth wakens before my wondering eyes.

I gaze on rebirth, new birth, blossoms and buds.

My faith deepens. These are gifts from paradise.

The day sparkles ~ Blue skies, green grass, a robin's song!

A soft fragrant breeze tenderly caresses me.

What have I done to deserve all these pleasures?

Money can't buy them. God gives them to all; they are free.

TRIBUTE TO A RETIRING MINISTER

JULY 10, 1986

"There is a season for everything-
Each purpose beneath the sun".
With these words our pastor told us
That his season at Central was done.

For ten long years he labored hard
Bible knowledge to impart.
He trained our minds in wisdom's ways;
Put love in every heart.

He served us well for all that time
On call both night and day.
He taught God's Word and fitted us
To find life's better way.

Wherever needed he was there.

His aid was at our command.

He prepared us for life's battles fierce,

Ever ready with a helping hand.

He visited the sick and sorrowful.

To all he's very dear.

He helped us with living and dying;

'Twas good to know he was near.

He laid foundations sure and strong

On which to build a life.

That at some future time will shine

And triumph over strife.

His shepherding us from day to day

Has knit us in a tie.

Of friendship, kindness and good will

Which time will sanctify.

We may not ever meet again

There's only One can tell,

But what God does is always best

Our pastor taught that lesson well.

The time for last goodbyes draws near,

But before our friend departs,

Our thanks to God for Reverend Keach
We give with all our hearts.

SILENTLY

Though not one word is spoken aloud,

We often talk together, God and I.

His thoughts like the wind blow across my
mind,

He knows my soul – He hears every sigh.

Today I followed a forest path

And listened to tunes of woodland song
birds.

God's voice was in their sweet melodies.

There was more than music, I heard His
words.

"I love you! I love you! I want you to know,

I'll always be with you, wherever you go."

That night in bed I questioned myself,

Were they really God's words I heard today,

Or was it all an old women's dream,

Had my imagination gone far astray?

CHAPTER FIVE

CARDS CREATE CONNECTIONS

RECYCLED CARDS

I treasure the cards my friends send me

And I hate to throw them away,

So some have been resurrected

To live another day,

Dear friends for whom I remake cards

Are with me while I cut and glue.

In fancy we're together again

Back to some golden days we knew.

This card is yours, so for a while

I'll be spending time with you.

Recalling things we used to say

And doing things we used to do.

Some folks say my collection is junk.

Now that certainly is not true!

Cause with each card from some
cherished friend

I'm keeping precious memories too.

CHRISTMAS LETTERS

CHRISTMAS 1993

Anyone who has lost a loved one finds lots
of sad spots in the holidays. Thoughts of
lots of those gone before always hover
around. When we stop to think what
Christmas means - things get happy again:

Christmas is a time for joy

Shared with friends and family.

I'm a bit sad - faces are missing

From the group gathered around the tree.

Their voices I won't be hearing

With carolers making merry today.

I long for their smiles, the touch of their
hands.

Some tear drops escape. I wipe them away.

Beneath the tree is a manger scene.

There's Mary and Joseph and their little boy.

He is Christ that died that we might live.

Surely, tears today, should be tears of joy.

The cross, the empty tomb, mansions on
high -

I ponder some things, the Christ child
brings.

Our loved ones are at peace - home with the
Lord.

Let bells ring; carols pour forth; my heart
sings.

CHRISTMAS 1996

John will be eighty years old at the end of this year and the kids are already forming committees, planning a big party. A hall has been reserved and the children plan to have the event catered so everyone can be free to mingle with the guests and enjoy.

Soon I will be eighty too. I love it!!! God pours his treasures and beauty into every season of the year and into every season of life. I feel a bit smug about my age – like I have been especially blessed. Seems there is a little adventure around every corner.

Some of them are sad adventures, but lots are happy ones.

John is working downstairs and is calling for me to come and see something. So I go to obey his bidding.

****

I have returned. The above line represents approximately four hours and you could never guess what we were doing. I got my Christmas present and I drove it to Buckland Mall to try it out. It is a 1991 Plymouth Acclaim, white. Like I said, life is certainly great with surprises around every corner.

We had been talking about going on a cruise

and I made the remark that the only objection I had to a cruise was that after two weeks there would be nothing to show for it except some photos, a tan and five or six extra pounds. John took me seriously so there is my cruise! Of course, there are taxes and insurance that I carefully avoided mentioning.

Merry Christmas. The day when blessed joy is known throughout the earth as happy people everywhere observe the Christ Child's birth.

I can't seem to concentrate. Think I will go out and "burn some rubber".

CHRISTMAS 2000

The ambers in the fireplace are burning brightly and I am sitting in the comfy sofa chair watching the flickering shadows on the walls and the ceiling. John is busy in his workshop and I am alone, but not for long because I am going to visit you tonight, in spirit, while I convey to you my Christmas greetings in this letter.

I'll search my memory for the events of summertime that bear recalling. Just the mention of "summer" and skies become blue and sunny, birds fly aloft, grass is green and soft flowers are everywhere. My 82nd

summer was as beautiful as God intended.

Of course, into every life some rain must

fall. My "rain" being the eye operation

which plagued me for months. Even now

sutures keep popping up from time to time

and must be removed. The doctor says that

sutures may appear occasionally for the next

year. A nice, young anesthetist held my

hand. At the end of the operation I said it

would have been nice if I had a picture;

something for memories and smiles at some

day in the future. From somewhere he

produced a camera. I don't have to wait for

the future, it is something to laugh at right now.

Though my Christmas shopping is done, I love to go to the malls, just for the fun of it all. There are carols in the background in all the stores, evergreen trees with baubles on strings, twinkling bright lights, shining toys, pretty dressed dolls in bonnets and lace, tempting gifts of all kinds. I just smile at every one and get a smile and a "Merry Christmas" in return. I walk around with the crowds with a feeling of peace, goodwill and mostly of love and joy.

Our tree stands straight and tall in the corner of the front room. It is artificial, but I spray the rooms with a pine scent and it really does look and smell real. I like when daylight ends and I sit with my "slippered" feet, nice and warm on the couch and I bask in the beauty of it all. The Christmas tree is decked with bright ornaments and tinsel and the flickering lights cast weird shadows on the walls and ceiling. I sometimes go back to the long ago and feel like a little girl again and my heart beats fast at the thought of the approaching holidays.

It is a grand time of the year that brings the children home all at the same time with their children and their children with their children. Happy days with the kitchen filled with the aroma of cookies and breads, pies, cakes, all kinds of goodies. Everyone has secrets and bright packages and smiles and hugs and kisses.

All of this for the Christ Child's birthday, many years ago and many, many miles away, started. I have shopped and sewed a lot. I sit amid all of my decorations and purr with contentment. Maybe this is what

people call a "second childhood". How I

love it, no matter what it is called.

CHRISTMAS 2013

Another year is nearly over and Father Time has been active – scribbled his signature all over my face; made my step a bit more feeble and slow; and robbed me of my failing eyesight. I had glaucoma, but got macular degeneration also and have been declared "legally blind". I can see about two feet, but am in a thick, gray fog. People are shadows with no faces; I can read and write with a large magnifying glass with an LED light. My eyes get watery and blurred so I can't read or write long without a rest.

Mashed potatoes on a white plate are a challenge. I'm always trying to spoon-up the plate and come up empty or if the plate has a design, I try to mistakenly spoon up the design…very frustrating!!

The Department for Help for the Blind sent me some advice to help the blind, plus some pretty good, useful "stuff". There is a white cane (4" of red at the bottom). Personally I hate canes – I think they make me look pitifully decrepit, but with this one, a bit of red ribbon wrapped around it makes it look like a Christmas cane candy decoration and livens up the place and makes me look festive. There is a 1 ½" x 3" clock that tells time vocally at the push of a button, and a tape player that plays entire books. I have a list of about 1,000 books from the

Government Library and the Post Office delivers and returns are just put in the mailbox.

I began early celebrating the birth and life of Jesus. I love Christmas and intend to squeeze out every minute of its joy that I can hold. My tree was up and decorated the end of October and my

doorways are slowly being decorated by the arriving Christmas cards.

I love nights when I can't sleep! I sing hymns out loud, make up poetry and letters mentally. I love to take strolls down Memory Lane. I can always find my darling John somewhere on Memory Lane waiting for me. John, my children (all senior citizens now) and I have made wonderful memories together.

You've heard about "Queen for a Day". Well, I'm "Queen" every day. All my children are good cooks, even my son. I love "old age" and much of the reason is because of them. Surprises are waiting around lots of corners. Another little guy joined our family, making me a great, great grandmother – five generations – makes me feel very special. Most people don't get to know the joy.

See, you give a woman a chance to talk and she never stops. I have written an autobiography. My daughter, Margaret, has offered to type this letter and I have accepted so you can read it.

I love writing "Christmas Keep in Touch Letters". It sets my heart aglow with the joys and memories of olden, golden yesterdays. "Nighty Night – Merry Christmas. It is way past my bedtime and I am getting tired, so off to bed and pleasant dreams of Christmas."

God Bless,

CHRISTMAS 2014

2014 has led me to be a "published author". After visiting the Windsor Historical Society, touring the Captain Howard Home and holding his pocket watch, I entered a contest. My submission placed among the five to be published on the internet. Popular votes were then tallied. Yes, second place attained. Now I am invited to celebrate by meeting my fellow writers at a reception. All this and a cash prize, too!

My writing gave me the opportunity to sense the gratitude I feel for having lived in Windsor more than sixty years. Raising five children on a farm and sharing many blessings in our first home. Then on to the years John and I enjoyed retirement on Timber Lane, where I continue to be loved

and cared for. Wishing you and yours a
blessed, peaceful Christmas and happy,
healthy New Year.

CHRISTMAS 2015

It is the Christmas Season again. Time to get in touch with dear folk whom we have neglected, but don't want to lose. There have been no grand cruises, no exotic vacations. But sometimes things at home can be even more interesting. Old age is not all swallowing pills and visiting doctors.

Tonight's sky is aglow with red and gold from the sunset, marking another day coming to an end. My heart, too, is all aglow with the joy this day has brought.

It was a day of setting up the Christmas tree, decorating it and the house. My senior citizen children began work early with the background of Christmas carols. In a few hours they asked for silence. I heard a click, followed by "OH's, AH's and applause. I knew the tree was trimmed and lit.

I placed a remembrance plaque on the tree. This was my 97th Christmas tree and the thought filled me with awe and reverence. I considered what the birth of Christ meant to me and the world. I thought about Jesus's life, the cross, the empty tomb and felt a tingle and a thrill.

My children helped me with my mailing list. With each name that came up we unwrapped some happy memory, we laughed and talked about the old days. By midafternoon the house was filled with the aroma of cookies and other goodies.

It is now evening. I forgot to take my pills this morning. I didn't take my three hour nap. My tummy is filled with lots of NO,

NO's and a few Tums! I should feel old and pitifully decrepit, but I feel like a teenager again and hate to go to bed and leave it all behind.

A delightful day is over. I am glad you have been a part of my life ~ thanks for the memories.

Wishing you and those you love a very Merry Christmas and Happy New Year.

CHRISTMAS 2016

For months my children have been begging me to get a hearing aid, but because of my advanced age I refused. I felt they probably would not get their money's worth. How much longer can I live? However, they came up with a good reason why I should have them. They are tired of yelling at me and the five of them would chip together and give the aids to me as a Christmas present.

My children gave me my Christmas present early. Unless you have been saying, "Huh?" after nearly every sentence directed at you; you have no idea what a wonderful gift hearing aids are. I love them. How did I ever enjoy living without them?

Recently I woke up in the middle of the night. My talking clock indicated it was midnight. I just laid there alone with my thoughts and thought about the happiness my hearing aids had brought. I got up and stood beside the bed; named my kids one by one; and applauded. Just my way of giving them a standing ovation! Then I went back to bed and to pleasant dreams.

Margaret gives me my shower every week. Micki and Johnnie rake and bag leaves, keeping the yard park-like;

while Johnnie's wife, Wendy keeps me company. Esther is a nurse. Our doctor! Jeannette just returned to Florida from being with me for three weeks.

I will say, "Merry Christmas" and hand my typed draft over to Margaret to correct the typing mistakes and mail.

CHRISTMAS 2017

A CHRISTMAS GRACE

Almighty God, we have gathered today to celebrate the gift you gave to the world…your Son, Jesus. We thank you for the way he has changed our lives and given us hope for a better world.

Christmas is a time for giving and sharing. We are happy to be together to share the delicious food before us.

Thank you for Christmas.   Amen

Christmas blessings can be many,
Our hearts filled with joy.
If we remember to fix our sight,
On that small, blessed boy.

CHAPTER SIX

WRITING IS WONDEROUS

WINDSOR HISTORICAL SOCIETY CONTEST

"Time to get up Mom. Time to see Captain Howard's pocket watch. If you want to enter the contest, we have to get started."

My answer was "I've changed my mind. I feel depressed, blue and I am tired of taking a bushel of pills every day! I am tired of being blind and being 96 years old. Pocket watches are things for men and they really don't interest me."

I could hear the heavy rain on the window pane, just the fitting weather for the mood I was in.

My daughter reminded me of all the good things Windsor has to offer, the Senior's

"90's club", the library, music, arts, restaurant's, activities on the green, the Windsor Historical Society, etc. The writing contest was one more example of creative activities that Windsor had to offer. With her prodding, I got up, and I may not like men's watches, but I did like the idea of contest prize money.

We went to the Windsor Historical Society and the tour guide put the watch into my hand after stating some historical facts.

I felt a tingle and a bit of a thrill as the feeling of depression and self pity of the morning was lifted while she acquainted me with the owner of the watch, Captain Howard.

The tour was delightful and the time passed quickly. We spent a couple of happy hours, met a few friendly folks that I may never meet again, but they had left me with a nice memory and a smile on my face.

That night back home alone with my thoughts, I decided to enter the contest after all. I had changed my mind about pocket watches. I felt they were fascinating, interesting and some come with adventure stories.

Captain Howard traveled to faraway places like the East Indies and England to buy goods for his wife's store. His watch and the tour opened the door to a new world of historical Windsor that I hadn't been to before and want to know more about now.

Windsor was good to the Captain. He was a prosperous man. He was part of the upper class as indicated by having been able to afford a pocket watch.

Windsor has also been good to me for the past 60 years. No place on earth do I love more than the dear, pretty town of Windsor.

This is the place that helped my husband and me to raise our five children into kind, caring adults, who also prospered from their life in Windsor.

It had been a beautiful, happy, memorable day. I find that most Windsor days are like that.

October 2014,   SECOND PRIZE

TICKLE MY FUNNY BONE

Dear Grandson Tommy,

My last birthday was my 80th. I am finding out that the 80's are a funny time of life. I mean "funny-ha-ha" as well as funny peculiar. I'll give you an example:

Our old ladies' circle had a meeting last week to which we invited another old ladies' group from another town.

We served a delicious lunch and their leader gave a lovely speech. There were three ladies, plus one man. One of the ladies from the other group had her husband with her which seemed strange at the time, but I found out why later.

After the nice speech from Marie, this lady, Jane, whose husband was with her, stepped up to the podium stating that she wanted all of us to be aware that baking soda was very valuable for other purposes beside eliminating refrigerator odors. She used it regularly to erase wrinkles; also to cure rashes, etc.

She said that she discovered the most important application when she had pneumonia a few weeks ago. It seemed she added water, made a paste, and smeared it all over her body.

This last statement proved too much for my sense of humor and a small giggle escaped. I quickly covered it up with a pretended cough and my hankie.

I looked around and no one was even smiling. Questions flooded my curious mind. How did all these ladies manage to keep straight faces? Was it sympathy, politeness, or were they seriously planning to embalm their bodies with baking soda sometime in the future in case of an attack of pneumonia and needed details in the form of a recipe?

I found myself wondering about how many boxes of baking soda were needed for her illness and what was the total cost?

She was going on and on and my glee was getting more intense. I tried to think serious thoughts like "This could be me in a couple of years or maybe in a couple of days. Even that seemed funny. I left and got a drink of water to gain control.

When I returned, Jane's husband had her safely and quietly seated by this side. Her husband had come for a purpose. He was obviously aware that baking soda didn't cure all of Jane's problems.

Next time I write I will be a "nice" person and more serious.

Love, Grammie

GETTING ACQUAINTED

Dear Tom,

Margaret said it would be nice if you and I could meet,

When I heard you were a scientist I got cold feet.

I stand in awe of scientist, don't have a clue,

What a little old lady like me could say that would interest you.

Our meeting would be a disaster,

Scientific conversation I never could master.

We have nothing in common, you and I,

We would sit in awkward silence with nothing to say, but "Goodbye".

We did have our meeting, you brought a lovely surprise;

Flowers, Thanks, Scientists are charming guys.

Let me thank you for your valentine here and now,

Munson's mints, how sweet of you-yummy, gee, wow!

Our conversing was scintillating,

Mentally, I thought it was elevating.

I found you easy and comfortable to talk to,

Not one awkward silence the whole visit through.

I'm glad we met, 'Twas a really delightful day,

May I call you my friend, I'd like it that way.

WE MET

We were worlds apart-an ocean between

Your home was Scotland; mine the USA.

In spite of obstacles you came my way

By some miracle, one Sabbath day.

When your Dad lost his job, he decided,

America is the place to be.

Here in the US we met suddenly.

You went to Sunday school; sat next to me.

A blue eyed, red headed, freckled faced lad,

You turned, a big smile for me, and said,
"Hi".

I recall well the boy you used to be

Though eighty-three long years have gone
by.

GONE NOW

Gone now are the buildings that sheltered
our childhood;

Torn down to make way for more modern
things.

Where are the friends who shared our school
days?

Gone too soon – the flutter of butterfly
wings.

Poets would say we're in life's sunset.

That's a nice way of saying, "We're old".

All things come home to rest at sunset

And the lovely day ends in a blaze of gold.

GRANDMA'S MIND WANDERS

TO MICHELLE AND DAVE

Soon I'll join the celebration,
As in beauty you walk down the aisle.
I know my thoughts will wander a bit
At least for a little while.

I'll think of the time your Mom and Dad
Put a blanket of pink in my arms-
A dream come true! A sister for Dawn!
We're still awed by your baby-sweet charms.

I touched your tiny, fuzzy head.
Wee fingers clutched my fingers too.
We rocked and cuddled and loved that babe.
Our lives were full of you.

My kids and grandkids are the smartest.

They're more beautiful than any other.

Search the world, you'll find they're the best.

I'm a pleased, proud Mom and
Grandmother.

Grandmas see things that no one else can.

At the end of the aisle there's a gate

That, hand-in-hand, you and Dave will pass
through.

To a land where great treasures await.

I pray that your fondest dreams come true

As you travel life's unknown way.

And all your joys be everlasting

Like the love you pledge on your Wedding
Day.

CONGRATS-YOU ARE SEVENTY

Dear Tom,

I got this news from Margaret.

Wish I had a present, but don't know what to get.

I'd have to take on a job to give you what I want to buy.

I want the biggest, most expensive, the best,

Because you are my kind of guy.

But, wait, it's not the size or cost that counts,

It's the thought that matters they say.

I am going to send some thoughts of you

That came into my mind today.

Margaret bought me half a typewriter,

She said half is better than none,

Believe me half a typewriter

Is not the tiniest bit of fun.

But you bought the other half and came to
my rescue,

It was a kind and caring thing to do

For an old lady that you hardly knew.

A whole typewriter gift is precious

I'll never tire of thanking you two.

One night you came for supper

And gave us a big surprise,

You, a man of science,

Washed dishes before our eyes.

You were an inspiration to behold,

A treasure rare, though a wee bit old.

142

COLONOSCOPY

What a scary word. "Colonoscopy".

I wanted to hide! I'm too old to run!!

I went to CTGE and very soon learned

The scary word was <u>almost </u>"fun".

The kind, caring staff had plenty of smiles.

I had no smiles, so the staff gave me some.

The genius doctor was skillful and
charming.

I felt like a queen, so grand was my
welcome!

I went to sleep painless; woke up the same.

Tasty pastry and juice left a cherry glow.

The only pain I felt was in my heart,

When someone said, "It's time to go."

AN AFFAIR I'LL REMEMBER

I'm thinking, John, as we travel home.
We didn't leave the party behind.
It's recorded from start to finish
On the VCR tape of my mind.

What an awesome celebration!
I still feel the tingle and thrill!
I touch memory's play-back button
And re-run glad moments at will.

Again I savor the gift of love
From our children who planned it all.
They created a dazzling ballroom
For a dark, dingy rented hall.

They cooked a banquet, invited friends
To be a part of our happy day.

How it warmed our hearts to see them!

We hugged, we laughed, and we wiped tears away.

The romantic tunes we danced to

Opened floodgates of memory

And turned back clocks to the "good old days"

When dreams were young and so were we.

I saw the church, the school, my home.

I could smell Mom's fragrant pies.

Folks said we were poor. I felt rich.

I owned all the stars in the skies.

I like thinking of the boy next door;

Sunday picnics shared in the park;

The sweetness of stolen kisses

On the back porch stairs after dark.

Our party took a year to produce-
Speeches, flowers, balloons, candle light.
Guests oh'd and ah'd the homemade cake.
We dined in elegance that night.

Goodbye time was a grand finale-
Confetti showers and good- will cheers.
Our car was trimmed with streamers of
white
And a sign, "Married Just 50 Years".

SUMMER TREASURE

When winter comes; when trouble strikes;
And tears get in the way;
'Tis then my precious memories,
Return to cheer my day.
I'd like to share my treasurer
From a summer that was, oh, so good!!
My Honey and I saw new places
And ate lots of tasty food.

We chatted with many friendly folk,
They're never hard to find.
Tho' I don't expect we'll meet again,
They left some smiles behind!
We saw the sun set; we saw it rise;
Went walking in the rain.
We did a lot of great-fun-things;
I'd like to do again.

We wandered down a country lane,

I picked a bright bouquet.

From an apple tree a yellow bird

Sang sweetly a roundelay;

On a sunny slope we sat and walked;

The billowy clouds float by.

Misty, blue mountains towered aloft,

Their summits touched the sky.

We loitered in a covered bridge

And waded an ice-cold stream.

God seemed so near we took time out

To meditate and dream.

Of the One who formed those mighty hills

Huge stars in the midnight blue.

Who promised greater things await

When our time on earth is through.

I've told just a few adventures

Of a summer gone by too fast.

There's a little more I'd like to add,

I've saved the best 'til last.

My nicest memory ----------

Whether near or far I roam,

Is when my ship drops anchor,

In the peaceful port called "HOME".

HOME IS WHERE THE HEART IS

It makes no difference where I wonder or
roam.

There is no place like the old place that I call
"home".

John and I love it here, it's our joy and pride.

It's the love nest we dreamed of when I was
his bride.

Just a humble abode on an acre of land,

Plain and simple, in our eyes it's simply
grand.

It's got tomato plants, tree, songbirds and
flowers.

A nice yard and porch where we spend
happy hours.

A house needs children, we dreamed of
three or four

We had five, they multiplied into lots more.

Now there's grandchildren, great grands too,
quite a few-

Lovelier than we reamed, our dreams came true!!

Children haunt this house when twilight shadows fall,

Eating cookies, slamming doors, outside playing ball.

Little ghosts from yester years, how I love you all.

Small rascals leaving crayoned artwork on the wall.

This sturdy structure is old now and so are we,

But it still protects and shelters great granddad and me.

The old homestead calls me back when I go roaming,

I hear it day and night until I am homing.

SUMMARY

Are you afraid of the dark?

With vision so stark?

A gloom developed in your view,

But I see a spark growing in you.

A light that shines brighter each day,

Clarity that helps illuminate my way.

A glittering spirit that is yours alone,

Born of your soul, deep in your bone.

My sense of sight, shows me a woman,

Loving, caring, an enlightened human.

You no longer see all the vivid hues,

But your heart is a rainbow through and
through.

Will you take a walk with me?

A foggy, warm day by the sea.

We'll smell the salty air, mother and
daughter,

Listen to the seagulls above the crashing water.

The lifting fog reveals heat from God's sun,

A day at the beach is always fun!

The tide is cold, the sand forgiving,

Tasting the spray, now that's really living.

I watch the sun drop into the sea,

You know it's gone down, "It's gotten chilly".

As we walk off the beach in the shadows of night,

We are both led by your ever present light.

Are you afraid of the dark?

With vision so stark?

Scary as the dark might seem,

Your essence is a guiding beam.

Love, Margaret

July 2013

Made in the
USA
Middletown, DE